Upholstery
Basics & Repairs

RON PULTAR

D1331826

MINI · WORKBOOK · SERIES

MEREHURST

CONTENTS

Bridge chair (top left), occasional tub chair (top right) and ottoman (bottom).

Upholstery basics

Upholstery is a craft that had its origins in the sixteenth century and its purpose has changed little since then. With the modern materials available today and the techniques that have developed, upholstery projects and repairs can be successfully made at home.

Repairing or re-covering a piece of furniture with new upholstery is easily accomplished. It can be a lengthy process, but the rewards are definitely worth the effort and the satisfaction is so much greater when the work is your own.

If you have never done upholstery work before, start with a simple project such as a kitchen chair with a drop-in seat, an ottoman or maybe a footstool. These projects require the fewest tools and materials, are quick to complete, and are ideal for learning the various upholstery techniques such as fitting and stretching covers.

As you work on more projects, the techniques will become easier and you should be able to apply them to any upholstered piece, helping to transform your furniture.

Antiques require special restoration work, but older-style chairs like this one are not difficult to upholster at home using a few modern techniques.

PLANNING YOUR PROJECT

Before starting an upholstery project, it is essential to assess the individual furniture piece and plan the stages of work. Every project has different requirements. Some will only need re-covering, others may need frame repairs or new foundations. By planning your project in the following way, you can work out which techniques you need to apply to your project and what materials will be required.

Buttoning is a traditional upholstery technique which is easily done at home and adds an elegant finish.

METHOD

1 Assess the piece to be upholstered by looking at it critically and finding ways of improving it. Sit on it if you can, feel the stuffing with a flat hand to find any unevenness, and look for the areas that might need attention.

2 Strip off the old covers and wadding. Write down the order in which you take off the fabric pieces as you remove them so that when the time comes to re-cover the project, you can start from the bottom of your list. Also note the way the covers went on, for example, how many pleats were on a corner. Sketches, too, will help greatly. Keep all the old covers as a reference to assist you when you are cutting the new fabric, especially if fitting and sewing is involved.

3 After removing the old covers and the stuffing, assess the project's foundations for any repairs or reinforcements that may be required.

4 Check the frame for weak points. Place tension on the wood joints to ensure that the frame can withstand re-upholstering. If the frame requires repairs, polishing or painting, it should be done at this stage.

5 Assess the stuffing and decide if you will re-use any of the old materials. Then replace or renew the stuffing, in preparation for covering.

6 Cut out the new fabric covers. Refer to your notes, sketches and the old covers to assist you—a cover plan is useful, too.

7 Fit the new covers. Depending on the project and the upholstery requirements, this may involve a combination of techniques such as sewing panels, fitting covers around chair legs, stretching techniques, back-tacking and slip stitching.

8 Finish off the project with buttons, decorative nails, gimp or piping if required, or simply close off the underside of the project by attaching some calico as a dust cover.

It does not take a lot of time, space or materials to re-upholster a set of dining chairs, especially if the foundations are in good condition. Simply by changing the covers you can transform an old table setting into a fresh new one.

Work area, materials and fabric

Most of the equipment used in home upholstery can be purchased from a local upholsterer or upholstery supplier and you might even have some of the tools already. The range of fabrics available to upholsterers is inspiring in itself.

WORK AREA

A comfortable and spacious work area is essential, especially for medium to large projects which can be very heavy. Ideally, your work area will include:

- a bench or trolley, approximately waist height, to place your tools on;
- a workbench, approximately 150 x 90 x 72 cm (about the size of a small dining table), or two wooden trestles (upholsterer's horses) to put your project on;
- a sheet of chipboard or plywood, approximately 150 x 120 cm, to place on the trestles or workbench for cutting out fabric. (Alternatively, you may choose to use a clean area on the floor.)

MATERIALS

The hardware and materials listed here are the most commonly used in upholstery at home. It is best to purchase these items from a local upholsterer because of the small quantities required.

TACKS

Tacks are short nails with sharp points and relatively flat heads. The most commonly used in upholstery are 9.5 mm tacks (normal size) and 16 mm tacks (long size). Tacks are supplied by weight.

STAPLES

The most commonly used staple lengths in upholstery are 6–8 mm (normal size) and 10–12 mm (long size). If your stapler cannot take the long staples, then you may choose to use 16 mm tacks instead. Staples are supplied in packets.

SEWING THREAD

Use cotton or polyester thread in a suitable colour. Standard, clothing-weight thread may sew upholstery fabric but will not last very long. Use a heavyweight or upholstery-weight thread or the heaviest thread your domestic sewing machine can take. You may also choose to take your sewing to an upholsterer for a fee. Thread is supplied by the spool.

JUTE MATTRESS TWINE

Jute mattress twine is a natural-coloured, thin twine used for sewing buttons, stitching springs and other stuffing stitches. Use no less than four-ply twine. It is supplied by the spool or metre.

JUTE WEBBING

A natural-coloured, woven webbing with no elasticity, jute webbing is most commonly used under coil springs where the webbing does not need to stretch. A width of 50 mm is most often used in upholstery. It is supplied by the roll or metre.

RUBBER WEBBING

Rubber webbing is made of synthetic and rubber components woven to form a webbing with elasticity. Combined with hessian, it is a common foundation in upholstery. There are various grades available—in general, use a firm grade for seat foundations and a grade with more stretch for chair backs. Use webbing that is at least 50 mm in width. It is supplied by the roll or metre.

HESSIAN

Hessian is a natural-coloured, open-weave cloth made from jute fibres. A hessian weight of 18 ounces is the most commonly used in home upholstery; 14 ounce hessian is used for more advanced upholstery. Hessian is used in upholstery foundations and also behind fabric panels for reinforcement. It is supplied by the linear metre.

FIBRE

A loose, teased blue-grey wadding made from shredded cloths, fibre (or flock) is used as stuffing over hessian on top of coil springs. Alternatively, some people choose to use hair for durable, quality work.

FELT

Felt is a thick layer of natural-coloured cotton fibres that is used over existing wadding or where only a small amount of stuffing is required. Felt is supplied by weight or roll.

FOAM

A synthetic product manufactured to have minute pockets of air, foam varies in quality, hardness and thickness. Foam foundations are common in modern furniture and thin layers of foam can be added to original padding that is in adequate condition. Foam is supplied by size and thickness or by sheets.

FOAM RATINGS

Most foam ratings consist of two numbers, for example, #30-200.

The first number is the weight of the foam per cubic metre and ranges from approximately 15 to 36. The higher the number, the more plastic and less air there is in the foam, producing a better quality foam that lasts longer.

The second number grades the hardness of the foam—the higher the number, the harder the foam will be. In general, the foam hardness rating for the back of a chair will be around 70 to 100 and the foam hardness rating for a seat ranges from around 100 for a soft seat up to 200 for a firm seat.

Manufacturers of foam use different colours in the various foams to identify the grades.

POLYESTER WADDING

This is a soft wadding used for stuffing or as padding under the fabric covers. It is supplied in sheets by the metre or as a loose fibre.

QUILTING

Quilting is a calico and felt material used on chairs between the cushions and the spring foundations. It is supplied by the metre.

SLIP-STITCHING TWINE

Very strong, thin twine made from linen and available in various colours, slip-stitching twine is used for concealed hand stitches where it is not possible to use a sewing machine. It is supplied by spool or metre.

DECORATIVE NAILS

These nails or studs have decorative heads and are available in various colours and finishes. They have many uses in the finishing of furniture and are supplied by quantity.

CONTINUOUS STUDDING

Continuous studding is a decorative finishing strip with the appearance of many studs. Every fourth or fifth stud has a hole where a single stud can be attached. It is supplied by the strip.

GIMP

Gimp is a decoratively woven, continuous band about 12 mm wide. It is used in the finishing of upholstery to hide raw edges of fabric. Available in many colours, it is supplied by the metre.

A woven band of fabric, gimp is a decorative finish that is especially suitable for older-style chairs.

JUTE PIPING CORD

Jute piping cord is a continuous cord, approximately 3–5 mm thick. It is used to create a neat, piped edge on cushioning and upholstery. Jute piping cord is supplied by the metre.

PLASTIC PIPING CORD

Plastic piping cord is a synthetic, continuous, plastic hollow tubing, approximately 3–5 mm thick. Used in fabric-covered cushions, it will often result in the cushion losing its shape due to the normal shrinkage of plastic. It is best used when sewing vinyl-covered cushions because vinyl also naturally shrinks with use. It is supplied by the metre.

BACK TACK STRIPS

These strips are approximately 16 mm wide and are used to create crisp, straight edges to panels that have been back-tacked.

EDGING ROLL

Edging rolls are used to create a smooth shape to upholstery edges, to prevent stuffing slipping over the furniture frame and to stop the hard edge of the timber cutting through the stuffing and the fabric cover. There are many different types of edging rolls but the two most commonly used are made of plastic (a hollow tube with a seam allowance coming out of one side) or paper (layers of thin paper covered with a synthetic cloth).

ZIGZAG SPRINGS

These are spring metal wires shaped into zigzags and used as an upholstery foundation. They are often cut to size and are supplied by the spring.

ZIGZAG SPRING CLIP

A metal clip used to attach zigzag springs and sold by quantity.

DOUBLE CONE SPRINGS

Double cone springs are made of shaped spring wires and are available in various sizes. These springs will outlast other spring foundations if attached correctly. They are supplied by the spring in inch sizes.

COIL SPRING SIZES

To calculate the correct spring height for a chair seat, measure the timber side rail of the seat and add approximately 60 per cent to the height. For example, a timber rail 10 cm in height, plus 60 per cent, results in a measurement of 16 cm or 6.4 inches (coil springs come in inch sizes). So you would need a 6 or 7 inch spring.

UPHOLSTERY FABRIC

Before purchasing upholstery fabric, you should consider its purpose, cost and suitability as well as the current trends. Fabric selection is very important with antiques and older style furniture (see table opposite.)

PURCHASING FABRIC

There are three main outlets where you can purchase upholstery fabrics.

- Most furniture retailers have a good selection of upholstery fabrics, although they are quite expensive.
- Bargain fabric shops often have discontinued lines or damaged stock, but you must consider its quality and suitability as well as its cost. In the case of damaged stock, you may require extra fabric so that you can cut around the flaws.
- Most upholsterers have a large selection of fabrics. You may be able to leave a deposit and borrow sample books to take home, or obtain technical advice on choosing fabrics.

TYPES OF UPHOLSTERY FABRIC

- Cotton is usually low in cost and available in many designs and colours printed on a 100 per cent base cloth. Cotton is only suitable for light to medium domestic use.
- Linen can be expensive, but it is very strong with excellent abrasive resistance. Most linens consist of a mixture of linen for durability and cotton for softness. Patterned linens are printed on the base fabric. Linen is suitable for medium domestic use and most types of upholstery.

FABRIC FOR PERIOD FURNITURE

PERIOD	TYPICAL COVERINGS	MOTIFS
Early Jacobean	Velvet, leather, linen, tapestry	Oak leaves, fruit, flowers
Late Jacobean	Cane, velvet, silk tapestry, elaborate trimmings	Leaves, flowers, birds
Queen Anne	Leather, wool, silk needlework	Scallop shells, leaves, flowers
Chippendale	French brocade, satin, tapestry, small floral or panel designs on a plain background	Detached sprigs of flowers, ribbons, knots, cupid's bows, medallions
Sheraton	Striped or flowered satin, brocade	Inlaid shells, flower swags and motifs
Regency	Striped satin, damask, brocade, velvet	Wreaths, floral swags, urns and vases

• Vinyl is a synthetic material that looks like leather at a fraction of the cost. There are many colours and patterns available. A practical cover with a waterproof finish that is easy to clean, vinyl can be uncomfortable in hot weather. Depending on the quality, vinyl is suitable for medium to heavy domestic use or commercial use. It is especially suitable for furniture on which spills are frequent.

• Jacquard fabrics mostly contain a mixture of cotton, polyester and nylon. There is an enormous range of designs and colours, and the patterns are woven into the fabric with fine threads so the colours can't be rubbed off as easily through wear. The better the quality of the fabric, the less transparent the jacquard will be. Depending on quality, jacquards are suitable for medium to heavy domestic use or commercial use.

Jacquard is excellent for upholstery work because the patterns are woven into the fabric with fine threads.

• Tapestry is a classic, very heavy, ornamental fabric which often has a pictorial motif illustrating a story. Tapestries are excellent for long-term wear and usually contain threads of cotton, linen and/or nylon. They are suitable for heavy domestic use but look especially good on antiques or traditional-style furniture.

• Velvet is a fabric with a thick, close pile. It is long lasting and comes in a variety of plains, floral patterns and cords. It is suitable for medium to heavy domestic use.

Stripping covers and stuffing

Remove the old fabric covers and stuffing from your furniture piece very carefully, especially if you intend to use the old covers as patterns or plan to re-use the stuffing. Work cautiously around decorative timber as it is easy to damage accidentally.

REQUIREMENTS

- Bent ripping chisel
- Regulator
- Side cutters or pincers
- Wooden and/or rubber mallet
- Medium-size hammer
- Medium-size chisel
- Coarse abrasive paper
- PVA wood adhesive
- Damp cloth
- Replacement dowel (if necessary)
- Dowel-sized drill bit and electric drill (if necessary)
- Clamps (for re-glueing if necessary)

STRIPPING THE COVERS

When removing tacks or nails, always work following the timber grain, never across the grain, as it is very easy to split the timber or chip off large pieces of wood. Look for the grain lines running along the show wood (see diagram page 13).

You must wear protective goggles when removing tacks and nails as it is possible that one may hit you in the eye. If you suffer from allergies, wear respiratory protection when removing stuffing.

1 To remove tacks or nails that were used to attach the old covers, place the flat end of the ripping chisel under the edge of the tack or nail and tap the end of the chisel with a wooden mallet.

2 While tapping the chisel with the mallet, lever the tack or nail upwards and, after a few firm taps, it should lift off quite easily.

3 To remove staples, force the regulator point under the staple and lever the regulator on the edge of the timber to lift the staple upwards. One end of the staple will remain in the timber. If you're pulling out staples next to polished timber, don't lever on the timber as it can be damaged. Place a thin, flat metal strip under the

1 Put the flat end of a ripping chisel under the tack or stud, tap with a wooden mallet, and lever upwards.

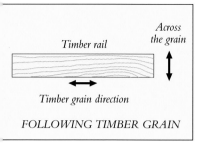

FOLLOWING TIMBER GRAIN

regulator and over the timber for protection and lever on the strip.

4 Grip the staple with side cutters or pincers and, with a twisting and pulling motion, pull the staple out of the timber. You might find that lifting several staples with the regulator and then pulling them all out with the side cutters will save you some time.

5 Mark the old fabric panels with their identifying name and a directional arrow so that you know where the panel belongs on the project (see page 17.)

6 Make sketches of the chair details. For example, draw the position of

pleats on the old fabric or sketch it on paper so that you can copy the original pleating when re-covering.

7 List the fabric panels as you remove them so that you can re-cover the project in the same order. When you start putting the new covers on, you can work from the bottom of the list to the top.

8 If you plan to re-use the old stuffing, it is important to keep it intact, so carefully place both arms under it and remove it cautiously. If you are not replacing or adding to the old stuffing and you do not need to work on the foundations, the area can be left alone until you are ready to re-cover it.

● Most stuffing is easily stripped but if the foam is glued down, use a fully extended trimming knife or a long, serrated knife to cut the foam from the foundation.

● If the fibre is held by twine (the bridle ties), cut the twine carefully with a trimming knife.

● Tacks or staples securing the stuffing will also need to be removed.

3 Force the regulator point under the centre of the staple and lever the regulator to lift the staple upwards.

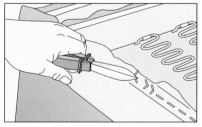

4 Grip the staple with side cutters or pincers and, with a twisting motion, pull the staple out of the timber.

Frame repairs

Checking and repairing the frame is a crucial part of upholstery. Most broken frames can be mended at home, but you may also take the frame to a cabinet-maker or upholsterer to repair.

CHECKING THE JOINTS

Most joints in modern furniture consist of two or three wooden dowels glued together with PVA wood adhesive. Tongue-and-groove joints or plain, glued joints held by staples or screws are less common. All come apart in the same way.

1 Pull the timber rails in various directions and, with your hand only, try to part the joint. If you can see or feel any movement at the joint, it is loose and will need repair. Proceed with caution as some joints have slight movement but are not ready to come apart. If you try to remove them with undue force, the dowel will probably break or split the timber rail, or the timber rail or leg may even snap in half.

CORNER BLOCKS

Many chair frames have a reinforcing corner block that must be removed before re-glueing the joints. Most corner blocks are glued and nailed, but if there are screws holding the block, unscrew them first.

2 Mark the top of the corner block and the nearby timber rail with a number to identify its position.

REQUIREMENTS

- Bent ripping chisel
- Wooden and/or rubber mallet
- Medium-size hammer
- Medium-size chisel
- Coarse abrasive paper
- PVA wood adhesive
- Damp cloth
- Replacement dowel (if necessary)
- Dowel-sized drill bit and electric drill (if necessary)
- Clamps (for re-glueing if necessary)

3 Place the flat point of the ripping chisel where one side of the block meets the rail and tap the end of the chisel with a wooden mallet to force the block away from the rail. Once the chisel is in as far as the bend, lever forwards and downwards to remove the block. If the block is stubborn when you lever it, remove your chisel or the chisel may snap. Hit the block hard with a mallet in a downward motion to detach it.

REPAIRING THE JOINTS

4 Place the chair on a workbench so the rail to be removed is horizontal but not resting on the bench. Hold

the adjoining rail in one hand and tap the horizontal rail with a rubber mallet downwards as close to the joint as possible. You may have to tap very firmly a few times before the joint parts. If the joint doesn't part after a few taps, do not proceed as the joint is not ready to come apart.

5 Mark the joint so you will know where to re-glue it. Sand or chisel off the old adhesive so that there is a flat end on the timber rail, with the clean dowels pointing out.

REPLACING BROKEN DOWELS

6 If a broken dowel is still in the timber rail, chisel the dowel flat so you have a level surface to drill on. Drill out the old dowel cautiously, making sure you don't drill right through the timber rail (a very easy mistake to make). Place masking tape on the drill bit to mark the depth.

7 Half fill the dowel holes on one side of the joint with PVA wood adhesive. Put in the new dowels and tap them in with a hammer. Clean excess adhesive with a damp cloth.

REPAIRING TONGUE-AND-GROOVE JOINTS

8 If you can part a tongue-and-goove joint without breaking the tongue, remove the old adhesive and re-glue the joint with PVA wood adhesive applied liberally. If the wooden tongue does break, make the surface flat and drill holes for dowels to replace the failed joint.

CLAMPING

9 Fill the remaining dowel holes with PVA wood adhesive so that the holes are about half to three-quarters full. Press the joints together by hand, wriggling them slightly to ease them into place. You do not have to push the joint together completely because the clamps will do that.

10 Place the project in the correct, upright position. Set the clamps on the joints and tighten each one as you position it. Replace any corner blocks. Wipe off excess adhesive and place the re-glued and clamped project on a flat surface so that it will remain square to the floor once the adhesive has dried.

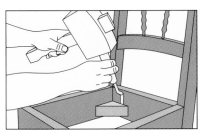

3 Place the flat point of the ripping chisel between the corner block and timber rail.

10 Set the clamps on the joints and tighten each one as you position it. Replace any corner blocks.

Measuring up

Careful measuring is essential to successful upholstery, especially with furniture that has many cover pieces. Always try to work to a method—start from the outside and work your way in or measure the largest panels first and work to the smallest.

MEASURING TECHNIQUES

On chairs with many panels, it is often easier to combine the stages of stripping the old upholstery with measuring up and cutting and fitting the new covers (see page 18). This technique is especially helpful if you are using the old covers as a guide.

ALLOWANCES

When measuring up your project, always include allowances for sewing and attaching the fabric panels.

• For panels that need attaching with tacks or staples, allow 50 mm of extra fabric on each side of the panel.

• For sewing seams, allow 12 mm of extra fabric on each side of the panel.

• Fabric for piping is cut 40 mm wide and fabric for double piping is cut 65 mm wide.

METHOD

1 Write down the name of the panel you are about to measure.

2 Place your tape measure on the fabric panel, first vertically and then horizontally (see diagram page 17). Don't forget to include sewing or tacking allowances where necessary.

• If you will be replacing or adding to the stuffing, it is best to re-pad the area first, then measure the panel. Alternatively, place your tape measure very loosely over the area that requires padding or work out the thickness of the stuffing and include it in your measurement. This ensures that there will be enough fabric to cover the repadded area.

• If you won't be adding more stuffing to your project, include an allowance of about 50 mm to each side of the panel for attaching.

• If you can't see the edges of the old panel while it is still in place and you aren't sure where it finishes, remove

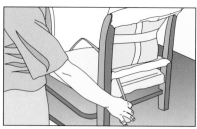

2 Place your tape measure on the fabric panel, first vertically and then horizontally.

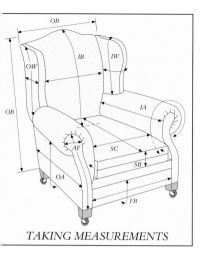

TAKING MEASUREMENTS

3 Write down the measurements next to the panel name and place a mark on the panel you have just measured so that you will not be confused about which panels you have done. Marking the panels in this way is especially important on furniture pieces with many cover panels that require sewing, such as a wingback chair.

4 Repeat steps one to three for each fabric panel on the project.

some of the outside fabric panels to look inside your project. (See instructions for stripping old upholstery on page 12.)

5 After you have measured all the panels on your project, draw up a cover plan so that you will know how much fabric you need to order for re-covering (refer to Cutting and fitting covers on page 18).

IDENTIFYING CHAIR PANELS

It is important to identify each cover piece by its panel name as you cut it out and mark the panel accordingly. This helps you recognise each piece as well as its position on the project, and provides you with a systematic approach to re-covering. You should also draw a directional arrow on the wrong side of the fabric panel as you cut it out to indicate which way the cover should be placed on the chair.

List the fabric panels as you remove them so that when it comes to re-covering the project, you can work methodically from the bottom of the list to the top.

ABBREVIATION	PANEL NAME
IB	Inside back
OB	Outside back
IW	Inside wing
OW	Outside wing
IA	Inside arm
OA	Outside arm
S	Seat
SC	Seat cushion
FB	Front border
SK (F,S,B)	Skirt (front, side, back)
SB	Side border
AF	Arm facing

Cutting and fitting covers

Making a cover plan is a crucial part of cutting and fitting covers as it helps you to calculate the amount of fabric you need. Take your time when cutting and fitting; it is essential to get it right.

COVER PLANS

A cover plan allows you to calculate the exact amount of fabric required for a particular project and plan how you will cut out the panels. This is especially important in furniture pieces with many upholstered panels to sew such as a wingback chair (see sample cover plan on page 19) or an occasional tub chair.

Some upholstery fabrics can be very expensive. In general they range from a few pounds a metre to a few hundred pounds per metre, therefore a cover plan is also useful in reducing the chance of costly errors.

Careful cutting and fitting of the covers is especially important with chairs that have many panels.

REQUIREMENTS

- Pen or pencil
- Paper
- Straight edge
- Large square
- Tailor's chalk
- Skewers or pins
- Sharp scissors
- Tape measure

SPECIAL FABRICS
Some types of fabric need special consideration when you are drawing your cover plan and cutting and fitting the panels.

• Fabrics with a pattern or motif should have the top of the motif closest to the top of the chair. The pattern or motif should be centred on the major panels and matched where possible when you are cutting the fabric. This ensures that the pattern or motif is displayed well and gives the project a professional finish. When calculating meterage for a patterned fabric, include any pattern allowances in your cover plan as necessary (see page 20).

• Velvet covers should have the pile running down the chair so that to brush against the pile, you will brush towards the top of the chair. When you are brushing against the pile on the chair seat, you will be brushing towards the back of the seat.

• Upholstery fabric is normally 137–142 cm wide. If the width of your upholstery fabric differs, take the measurement into consideration when drawing the cover plan.

DRAWING A COVER PLAN

1 Draw, to scale, the width of your fabric and use the length of the paper or graph paper as if it were the fabric roll. If your fabric has a pattern, roughly sketch it on the cover plan to help you match it on the panels.

2 Using your measurements, draw the individual panels to scale on your cover plan. Always draw (and later cut) the largest pieces first. There will often be enough space beside a large panel to cut out a small border piece or some other small panel.

3 Once all the panels are drawn, measure the length of the paper and reverse the scale to calculate the amount of fabric you require. If your fabric has a pattern repeat, use the pattern allowance table on page 20 to determine the amount of extra fabric needed for pattern matching.

MARKING OUT THE FABRIC

4 Working in a large area so that you can see most or all of the fabric roll, copy your drawings from the cover plan on to the fabric. Check for any flaws in the fabric and plan the panels

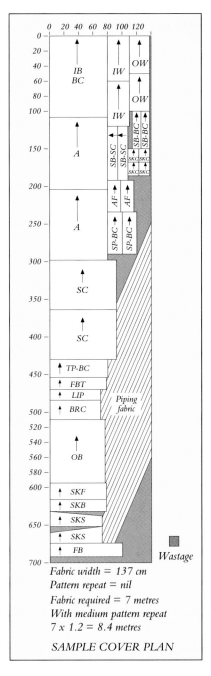

Fabric width = 137 cm
Pattern repeat = nil
Fabric required = 7 metres
With medium pattern repeat
7 x 1.2 = 8.4 metres

SAMPLE COVER PLAN

around them or use the flawed part in an inconspicuous area. When marking the fabric, keep the following points in mind.

• Always use tailor's chalk for marking so that mistakes can be corrected without wasting fabric.

• Never use a biro or felt-tipped pen to mark fabric as they are extremely difficult to remove. Ink can also bleed through to the face side of vinyls—a chemical reaction that can take up to six months to occur.

• Be careful as chalk marks can show through on lightweight fabrics that are white or cream-coloured.

• Always do as little marking as possible and try to mark the fabric on an outside edge of the reverse side.

CUTTING THE FABRIC

5 Cut the fabric ensuring that you cut the panels in the same direction following the thread line. Vinyl can be cut in both directions because there is no distinct thread line or pattern to it. Never cut out fabric with the reverse side facing you. As you cut, mark each piece with its identifying name and a directional arrow, using tailor's chalk on the reverse side of the fabric.

6 If your project involves many identical panels, such as a set of six dining chairs, cut the fabric for one chair first. Then, using the first piece as a pattern, lay the panel on the next part of the fabric you want to cut from. This method is especially useful for pattern matching.

ALLOWANCES FOR PATTERNED FABRICS★

PATTERN REPEAT	ALLOWANCE
Plain	Nil
Small, 0–10 cm	Nil
Medium, 10–30 cm	20 per cent
Large, 30–65 cm	30 per cent
Extra large, 65–75 cm	40 per cent

★ If you're unsure about the amount of fabric required, ask your fabric supplier whether you can purchase more fabric at a later date.

FITTING THE COVERS

7 Most chairs have symmetrical panels, in which case you should attach the panel to the chair with pins or skewers with the reverse side of the fabric facing outwards. Centre the motif if the fabric is patterned.

• If the panel you are fitting is not symmetrical, you should pin the cover on the project with the correct side of the fabric facing you and include the sewing or tacking allowance when you mark the shape with tailor's chalk.

8 *Once the fabric is positioned, mark the seam areas on the wrong side with tailor's chalk.*

• If there are timber rails, legs or any other details to fit the covers around, you may need to place cuts in the fabric so the panel is flat for marking (see page 42).

• Always measure the old fabric covers and the areas between the panels, for example between the two arms, to check that your chalk marks are accurate.

8 Once the fabric panel is positioned to your satisfaction, mark the seam areas on the reverse side with tailor's chalk, including allowances as necessary. Again, check every chalk mark is accurate.

9 Take off the panel and cut halfway around it, making sure you include any sewing or attaching allowances. If the panel is symmetrical, fold it in half on the axis and cut around the second side. This ensures the fitted piece is identical on both sides.

10 Lay the panel you have just cut on the project and check the fitting. Repeat the process for each panel of the project.

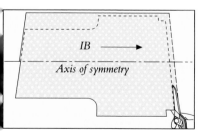

9 Take off the fabric panel and cut halfway around it, making sure you include any allowances.

CUTTING AND FITTING — ALTERNATIVE METHOD

Using the existing covers, you can also cut and fit the new fabric following this alternative method.

1 Carefully unpick the old panels with a trimming knife. Iron the panel with a warm iron, making sure the fabric thread lines are reasonably straight (do not use a hot iron on synthetic fabrics as the heat may melt the fibres). Lay the old panel on the new fabric and mark the shape with chalk.

2 Cut halfway around the new panel on the chalk mark. (The old panel will already have sewing allowances on it.) If the panel is symmetrical, fold it in half on the axis to cut the second side, to ensure the piece is identical.

3 Lay the panel you have just cut on the project and check the fitting of it. Repeat for each panel that requires fitting.

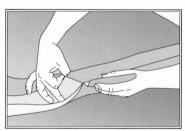

1 Carefully unpick the old fabric panels with a trimming knife. Iron the panel with a warm iron.

Sewing

Sewing is used for many aspects of upholstery; to join the cover pieces, to make the cushions and as part of the finishing techniques. The most common types of seams and stitching are easily accomplished at home.

STRAIGHT SEAMS

Use a straight seam for upholstery sewing with a stitch length of approximately 3–5 mm, depending on the weight of the fabric. Try sewing an offcut to determine the stitch length that best suits the fabric and to check that the machine is sewing correctly. Always include a sewing allowance of 12 mm unless otherwise indicated.

REQUIREMENTS

- Sewing machine with zip foot (see note on sewing machines)
- Heavyweight thread
- Small scissors
- Pins
- Tape measure
- Trimming knife (to unpick threads)

BACK-SEWN SEAM

This is a plain seam and the most commonly used in upholstery.

- Place the right sides of fabric together. Position them under the sewing machine foot with the edge of the fabric 12 mm from the needle.
- Sew the two pieces of fabric together, keeping the sewing allowance as even as possible.

SEWING MACHINES

A domestic sewing machine can be used for sewing light to medium weight fabrics, but for heavyweight fabric, piped edges or a double-piping, you will need an industrial sewing machine. Alternatively, you may choose to take your fabric to a local upholsterer for sewing.

TOP-STITCHED SEAM

Top stitching is used to reinforce a seam that will be under heavy stress.

- Sew the fabric together as for a back-sewn seam. Turn the panels over with the right side facing you and place them under the machine foot with the back-sewn seam about 3–4 mm from the needle.
- Sew the top stitch evenly distanced from the back-sewn seam and, while doing so, catch the two seam allowances of fabric neatly on the underside (see diagram on page 24).

TWIN-NEEDLE TOP-STITCHED SEAM

This stitch is normally performed on an industrial sewing machine that has

Some chairs require sewing only at the finishing stage, such as for piping and slip stitching. Others, like this wingback armchair, have many cover panels which require a combination of upholstery sewing techniques.

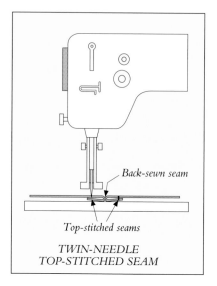

Back-sewn seam

Top-stitched seams

*TWIN-NEEDLE
TOP-STITCHED SEAM*

• Fold the edge of the fabric twice, making each fold about 12 mm wide. Place the folds under the sewing machine foot and stitch the hemline about 10 mm from the folded edge.

• When approaching a corner, stop sewing about 50 mm from it, fold the adjacent side of the fabric and continue sewing. At the corner, stop sewing and place the needle down through the fabric. Lift the machine foot and turn the fabric 90 degrees. Replace the foot and continue to sew along this side of the panel.

• To end the sewing, either run off the fabric panel (where applicable) or finish with a back stitch where you began the hem.

ZIP SEAM

Zip seams are commonly used on cushion covers. You can purchase a prefabricated zip or cut a zip about 50 mm longer than required.

• Fold under one edge of the zip fabric panel about 12 mm. Place the panel with the right side facing you over half of the zip. Sew together

two needles, but you can sew this seam on a domestic sewing machine.

• Sew the fabric together as for a back-sewn seam. Turn the panels over with the right side facing you and place them under the machine foot with the back-sewn seam about 3–4 mm from the needle.

• Sew the first top stitch row an even distance from the back-sewn seam, catching one side of the allowance on the underside of the fabric.

• Position the fabric under the machine foot with the other side of the seam under the needle. Sew the second top-stitched seam in the same way, while catching the other side of the allowance on the underside of the fabric.

SEWING A HEM

Hems are sometimes used to finish upholstery, such as on a chair skirt.

MATCHING PLEATS AND GATHERING

When sewing a cushion with pleated corners or gathering, sew the pleats or gathering on one panel first. Then, as you sew the two panels together, gather or pleat the opposite panel at the same point as the already sewn pleats or gathering to ensure that both sides of the cushion match.

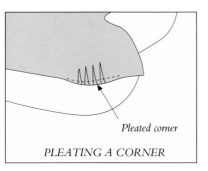

Pleated corner

PLEATING A CORNER

with a straight seam about 8 mm from the edge of the fold, ensuring there is enough room for the zip glide to pass the seam. Repeat with the opposite side of the zip.
• Put on the zip glide and sew the zip panel to the cushion border.

GATHERING A CORNER
Gathering a corner of a cushion cover with centre seams or centre piping ensures the cover fits neatly.
• Sew a line of straight stitches 6 mm from the edge of the fabric where you need to gather it.
• Pull one thread of stitches to create the gathering. Check the gathering on the project.

PLEATING A CORNER
Pleating on a corner of a cushion cover is an alternative to gathering.
• Mark the fabric edge where the pleats are to be sewn.
• Fold each pleat into place and sew in the pleats with stitch line 6 mm from the fabric edge.
• Check the fit of the pleats on the project. Pleat the opposite panel after you have sewn the panels together.

SLIP STITCHING
Slip stitching is a concealed hand stitch used to finish covers and close large pleats on upholstered furniture.

METHOD
1 Cut a length of slip-stitching twine. Tie two knots in one end and thread the other end through a small circular needle.

2 Slip stitches are sewn in the fabric folds. Starting from the inside of the fold on the first side, push the needle through to the outside of the fold. The knots will hold the thread inside the fold. Sew a stitch 5 mm long inside the fold on the second side.

3 Push the needle back into the first side, about 1 mm back from where the last stitch came out of the second side. Continue slip stitching in this way until you reach the end of the area to be sewn.

4 To finish, reverse the sewing for a few stitches then sew a few more forward stitches before cutting off the thread close to the fabric.

3 Push the needle back into the first side, 1 mm back from where the last stitch came out of the second side.

PIPED SEAMS

Piping provides a crisp, straight edge to upholstery coverings. Piped seams are also used to join fabric panels, especially if the join needs to be very strong. Piping fabric should be cut 40 mm wide. (For double piping finishes, see page 55.)

METHOD

1 Measure the length of the piped seam. Cut the cotton piping and the piping fabric.

2 Join piping fabric to obtain the required length by placing the right faces of the piping fabric together with the ends at 90 degrees to each other. Sew together with a diagonal back-sewn seam across the corner. Trim the excess fabric 12 mm from the stitch line. (See diagram.)

3 Sew the piping fabric around the piping cord using a zip foot on a domestic sewing machine or a piping foot on an industrial machine.

4 Sew the finished piping to one fabric panel, with the raw edges

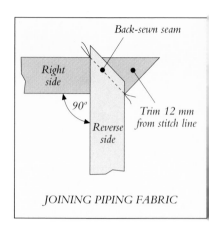

JOINING PIPING FABRIC

together and the right side of the fabric facing up. Include a 12 mm sewing allowance. If you have corners to sew the piped seam around, make small cuts in the seam allowance to assist with turning.

5 Place the next fabric panel on top of the other with the piping in between the two face sides of the panels. Sew together, making sure that this seam is closer to the piping than any of the others.

6 Turn back the seam and check that all the threads are covered up. If not, stitch again even closer to the piping to cover the other threads.

7 To join a piped seam, stop when approaching the ends of the piping and mark the piping fabric where the ends will meet. Sew the piping fabric together at this mark and cut the excess piping fabric and cotton piping. Then stitch the rest of the piping to the panels.

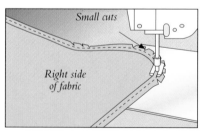

4 Sew the finished piping to one fabric panel with the right side of the fabric facing up.

SEWING A FULLY PIPED CUSHION COVER

Use these instructions to make a piped, separate cushion for a chair seat. A zip seam allows the cover to be removed for cleaning.

METHOD

1 Cut the zip fastener 50 mm longer than the finished size. Cut two face panels and the side border for the cushion cover. Sew the zip seam (see page 24), then the zip border section.

2 Cut two lengths of cotton piping to go around the cushion, including a 100 mm allowance. Join the piping fabric to obtain the right length. Sew the piping fabric around the cotton piping using a zip foot on a domestic machine or a piping foot on an industrial machine (see Piped seams).

3 Sew the piping to one face panel of the cushion with the raw edges

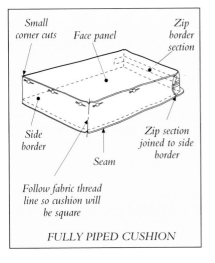

Small corner cuts
Face panel
Zip border section
Side border
Zip section joined to side border
Seam

Follow fabric thread line so cushion will be square

FULLY PIPED CUSHION

HINTS FOR SEWING

• Keep checking your sewing. Take the cover back to the chair or cushion at every stage to make sure that it fits correctly.
• Where possible, use the original cover as a reference.
• Pin the fabric panels together before sewing. Pinning cushions together before sewing helps visualise the finished item.
• When starting or finishing stitches, sew forwards and backwards to secure the thread.

together and the right side facing you. Include a 12 mm sewing allowance and place small cuts in this allowance to make cornering easier. Sew piping to the other face panel.

4 Join the zip section to one end of the side border panel. Starting here, sew the border to one of the piped face panels until you reach the other back corner of the cover. Work out the finished size of the side border and completely sew the zip section to the side border. Trim off any excess border fabric.

5 Follow the thread line from the face panel corners to the open side of the border and pin the corners of the second face panel and border together. Stitch the second face panel to the side border and zip part. Turn the cushion cover the right way out and check all the seams.

Stretching techniques

Stretching, the method of attaching soft materials to furniture, is one of the most important techniques to learn in upholstery. The same technique is used whether you are attaching fabric, hessian, foam or calico to chair seats, backs or arms.

REQUIREMENTS

- Foam: 12 mm thick; grade #24-160★
- Fabric
- Calico
- Tacks or staples

★ Materials given are for this particular chair seat.

STRETCHING DIRECTIONS

1 Mark the centre of each side of the fabric with a small nick, and mark the centre of each side of the timber frame with chalk or pencil. Match the marks to make sure the fabric will be square on the frame.

2 Gently pull the fabric over the seat at the centre of each side. Place a temporary staple or tack at each of these points. Then gently pull the fabric over the corner points and secure with temporary staples. Once the fabric is temporarily attached, you can staple the sides.

3 Beginning with one side and working from the centre temporary staple, firmly stretch the fabric over the edge of the frame and at the same time pull the fabric towards the corner. Staple into place about 25 mm from the corner. Repeat on the other side of the fabric. Pull out the temporary centre staple.

4 While stretching the fabric evenly over the frame, fill the area between the corner staples with permanent staples. It is very important to sight what you are doing to make sure the

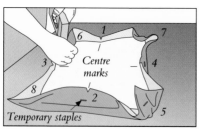

2 Gently pull the fabric over the seat at the centre of each side. Place a temporary staple at these points.

3 Stretch the fabric over the edge of the frame and at the same time pull the fabric towards the corner.

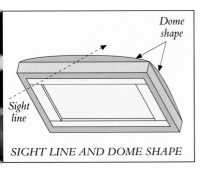

SIGHT LINE AND DOME SHAPE

tension on the fabric is even and creates a very slight dome shape to the seat (see diagram above).

• When you stretch foam over a seat that has fibre stuffing, such as coil spring seats (see page 36), there may be too much fibre on the outside edges of the seat. If so, pull a little fibre away from the sides and make sure that the remaining fibre does not lay around the outside of the timber frame. If the fibre is over the side of the frame, you will end up with an uneven edge along the seat.

5 Repeat steps 3 and 4 to attach the fabric to the opposite side of the seat, but use more tension when stretching the cover so that the stuffing is pulled down firmly and the cover will not be loose on the seat.

6 Repeat the procedure for the third and fourth sides of the seat, again using more tension on the fourth side. Once all the sides are permanently stapled, pull out the temporary corner staples. Finish off the corners with single pleats (see page 43) or double pleats (right).

DOUBLE-PLEATED CORNERS

1 Stretch the fabric over the corner and fold a pleat on either side of it. Make sure that both pleats are even on either side of the corner.

2 Permanently staple the corner between the pleats. Using scissors, cut the excess fabric from around the corner staple and the area where the pleats will be folded.

3 Pull one pleat down tightly, make sure it is flat and staple permanently. Staple any open areas next to the corner—you may need to pull out one or two side staples at this stage to ensure that the neat shape of the seat flows down to the corner. Cut off the excess fabric.

4 Pull down the second pleat and staple it over the first pleat. Again, you may need to pull out a few side staples to keep the dome shape of the seat correct. Cut off any excess fabric from the corner.

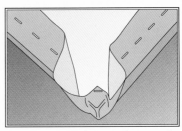

2 Permanently staple on the corner in between the pleats and cut around the corner staple.

The seat of this chair only needed an extra piece of firm foam and a new cover. A vinyl cover was chosen for easy cleaning and durability. With a coat of bright paint on the chair frame, the transformation was quick and complete.

Kitchen chair with drop-in seat

A kitchen or dining chair with a seat that drops into a timber frame is ideal for learning the basics of upholstery. The foundations of these chairs are usually made of foam, which is easy to replace, and the seat cover does not require any sewing.

REQUIREMENTS★

• Foam: 12 mm thick, grade #24-160

• Fabric: 0.5 m

• Calico: 0.5 m

• Tacks or staples

★ Quantities given are for this particular kitchen chair.

COVERING THE CHAIR

1 Strip off the old covers and foam foundation carefully (see page 12). Check the chair frame and repair and paint if required (see page 14).

2 Place the new foam on top of the seat frame and existing stuffing. Cut around the foam so that it is 7 mm larger than the frame on all sides.

3 Measure the chair seat and cut and fit the seat cover (see page 18). If the cover has a motif or pattern, make sure it is centred on the seat.

4 Stretch the new cover over the foam following the stretching technique described on page 28.

5 Finish the corners with double pleats and check that the drop-in seat fits neatly into the frame. Trim any excess fabric from under the seat.

CALICO DUST COVER

6 To finish the uncovered area under the seat, cut out a piece of calico approximately 25 mm larger than the area to be covered.

7 Position the calico over the uncovered area and fold the edges under. Place a permanent staple in the centre of each side of the calico.

8 Stretch the folded edges of calico from the centre staple towards the corners and staple the calico at the corners. Fill in the gaps between the centre and corner staples with more staples, making sure that the calico is evenly stretched.

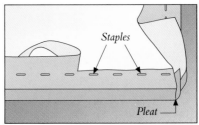

5 Finish the corners with double pleats and check that the drop-in seat fits neatly into the frame.

Ottoman

Upholstering an ottoman is an easy project that can be accomplished in a weekend, whether you are re-covering an old footstool or making a new ottoman like this one. Back-tacking is used to create a clean, crisp edge around the ottoman frame.

PREPARATION

1 If you are re-upholstering an ottoman, strip off the old covers and foundations and repair the frame if necessary. Or, you may choose to purchase a new ottoman frame like the one used here.

2 Attach new rubber webbing and hessian foundation (see page 35), and new plastic edging roll (see page 34.)

3 Place the 50 mm thick foam on the frame and make sure there is an even overhang on each side. Bevel the top and bottom edges using a trimming knife or long, serrated knife. Glue the foam on the hessian with a contact adhesive spray can. Then stretch the softer, 25 mm thick foam over the first piece of foam, creating a neat dome shape (see page 28). Staple the softer foam on the frame just below the edging roll.

COVERING THE OTTOMAN

4 Measure and cut the fabric (see page 18). Sew up the border and try it on the frame (don't include an allowance for the polyester wadding). Then sew the piping and attach the piping to the top edge of the border.

REQUIREMENTS*

- Rubber webbing (firm grade): 3.5 m
- 18 ounce hessian: 0.5 m
- 10 mm plastic edging roll: 1.8 m
- Foam: 50 mm thick, grade #29-200 (470 x 420 mm)
- Foam: grade #15-60 (600 x 450 mm)
- Fabric: 1.5 m
- Cotton piping
- Four back tack strips
- 200 g polyester wadding: 0.5 m
- Calico: 0.5 m
- Timber frame: 460 x 410 x 100 mm (optional)
- Four polished wooden cabriole legs: 150 mm in height (optional)
- Eight 50 mm chipboard screws (optional)

★ Quantities given are for this particular new ottoman.

5 Stretch the top panel over the foam and staple below the edging roll.

6 Fit the border piece back on the frame over the top panel and position it so that the piping is 5 mm below the unexposed plastic roll. Pull the border over the top of the stool

Timber frames, like the one used for this ottoman, are readily available to purchase and also easy to make. A traditional tartan fabric reflects the classic style and polished cabriole legs of this ottoman.

temporarily and place four or five staples into the piping seam allowance on each side of the frame to hold the border in place.

BACK-TACKING

7 Place a back tack strip over the seam allowance, with the top of the strip about 1 mm over the stitching

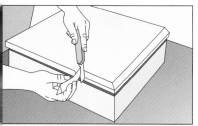

3 Place the 50 mm thick foam on the frame and bevel the top and bottom edges using a trimming knife.

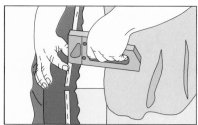

7 Place a back tack strip over the seam allowance, about 1 mm over the stitching line.

line. Make sure the border is evenly placed by measuring from the top of the back tack strip to the bottom of the frame, and maintaining that distance. Attach with long staples.

8 Pull the border back down and check that the border and piping are level. Undo some stapling if you need to fix any unevenness.

FINISHING

9 Staple the polyester wadding under the border over the back tack strips with normal-sized staples (6–8 mm) spaced about 25 mm apart. Then attach the bottom of the wadding with a few staples on each side. To join the wadding to go around the entire ottoman, butt the ends together—avoid any overlapping.

EDGING ROLLS

Edging rolls are available in various thicknesses and are used to create smooth shapes to upholstery edges.

1 Cut the end of the roll straight and position on the project. Make sure half to three-quarters of the roll hangs over the timber edge. Attach the roll with long staples or 16 mm tacks through the seam allowance. Pull the roll towards the corner and staple about 25 mm from the corner. Go back to the start and attach the roll evenly.

2 When turning a corner, place a V-cut with your trimming knife in the seam allowance and very

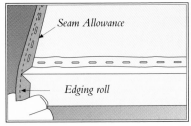

2 When turning a corner, place a V-cut into the welt and very slightly into the roll.

slightly into the roll. Turn the roll around the corner and tack in place.

3 To finish, butt the ends of the roll together. Staple a piece of fabric tightly around the join of the roll to prevent the ends showing.

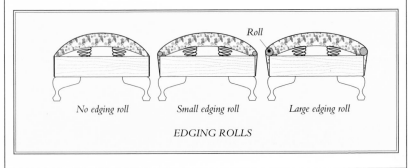

No edging roll   Small edging roll   Roll   Large edging roll

EDGING ROLLS

10 Trim the bottom of the wadding level with the bottom of the frame. Pull the border down over the sides and check the fit once more. Put a temporary staple in each corner to hold the stitch lines in place.

11 Ease the cover around the base of the frame and staple it to the underside with normal-sized staples, starting from the centre of each side and working towards the corners. Stop about 30 mm from each corner, pull out the temporary staple and then finish off the corner.

12 Stretch calico on the underside of the frame (see page 31).

13 Drill pilot holes into the cabriole legs, and screw the legs to the corners of the ottoman frame.

RUBBER WEBBING AND HESSIAN FOUNDATIONS

This technique for replacing or repairing rubber webbing and hessian can be used on all types of furniture with this foundation. You should only replace the rubber webbing if it is hard and no longer stretches, if it sags, or if there is not enough of it. Rubber webbing is fairly tightly woven, so it is not necessary to turn the edges back to avoid fraying.

1 Strip off the old webbing and note the amount so you can duplicate it. Add more webbing if necessary. If the gap between each web is more than 75 mm, the rubber webbing will not be durable.

2 Attach one side of the new webbing with a row of four long (10–15 mm) staples and a second row of three long staples. You can also use 16 mm tacks instead. Pull the webbing firmly across the frame and attach the other side. Use your trimming knife to cut the webbing

about 5 mm from the staples. Attach all vertical webs.

3 Attach the horizontal webs in the same way, but they should be interlaced with the vertical ones.

4 Attach the hessian with staples over the rubber webbing but leave it loose enough to compensate for sagging when the seat is used. Trim the hessian with scissors about 30 mm from the staples. Turn over the edges of the hessian and place more staples on top to prevent the edges from fraying.

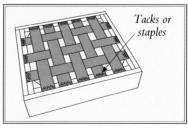

Tacks or staples

3 Attach the horizontal webbing making sure that you interlace them with the vertical ones.

Traditional dining chair

This technique for replacing or repairing coil spring seats can be used on any chair with this type of foundation. Coil springs last longer than any other type of upholstery foundation and should only be replaced if one or more of the springs are broken.

REQUIREMENTS*
- Jute webbing: 3.5 m
- Four 6 inch coil springs (use a firm grade, e.g. 9 or 10 gauge)
- Jute twine (for sewing springs)
- Cotton piping (for lacing springs)
- 18 ounce hessian: 0.5 m
- 10 mm plastic edging roll: 1.5 m
- Fibre: 1.25 kg
- Foam: 25 mm thick, grade #24–160
- Fabric: 1 m
- Calico: 0.5 m
- Tacks or staples

* Quantities given for one chair only.

PREPARATION
1 Strip off the old upholstery and stuffing (see page 12). Check the chair frame and repair it if necessary (see page 14).

REPLACING COIL SPRING SEATS
2 Remove the old foundations, including the springs, hessian, bridle ties and webbing, from the seat frame. Measure the underside of the frame and mark with pencil the position of the new webbing.

3 Attach the webbing to the furthest end of the seat with seven 16 mm tacks. Fold back to avoid fraying.

4 Stretch the webbing tightly across the frame with a web strainer and attach with four tacks. Cut the webbing 25 mm from the tacks, fold back and secure the folded section with three tacks. Repeat for each web, interlacing the horizontal webs with the vertical ones (see page 35).

5 Position the springs in the sitting area of the seat. Make sure the springs compress in a straight motion and that they don't touch each other.

6 Sew the springs into place with the packing needle and jute twine. Start and finish the sewing with slip knots

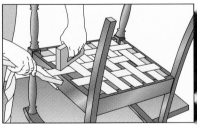

4 Stretch the webbing tightly across the frame with the web strainer and attach with four tacks.

This traditional dining chair needed new coil springs and stuffing in the seat. Fabric covers were chosen to complement the chair frame and the upholstery work was finished with a strip of decorative continuous studding.

and also sew about four slip knots to secure each spring to the webbing (see page 61). Lace all springs with cotton piping (see diagram page 39). Tie the cord to the springs with a clove hitch knot (see page 62) and attach the ends to the rails with clout nails. Make sure the springs are straight before you finish each knot.

7 Stretch the hessian tightly over the springs. Make small cuts to fit it around the timber rails if necessary. Fold back the raw edges and staple.

8 Sew each spring to the hessian with jute twine in the same manner as in step 4, but use a large circular needle so that you can hook around the spring through the hessian.

9 Attach the edging roll following the instructions on page 34.

SEWING THE BRIDLE TIES
10 Using a large circular needle and jute twine, sew the bridle ties very loosely so fibre can be pushed under them. Start with a slip knot, sew the first bridle tie around the perimeter about 50 mm from the outside and finish it where you began (see diagram opposite). Sew more bridle ties horizontally between the front and back ones. Sew the front and back bridle ties over the side ones, and centre ties under the side ones.

STUFFING COIL SPRING SEATS
11 Pick up handfuls of fibre and check for any lumps inside by teasing it with your hands. Starting at the front of the seat, push fibre under the centre of the bridle ties then slide the fibre to the outer edges. Keep packing in more fibre and pushing it to the edges until there is enough fibre under the bridle tie. Push the two quantities of fibre back to fill the hole in the centre. Repeat for the back of the seat, then the two side areas and lastly the centre bridle ties.

12 Push down firmly with flat hands all over the seat. Make sure it feels even and you can't feel the springs through the fibre when you sit on it. Place the foam on top of the seat and do a final check by sitting on the seat. Stretch the foam over the fibre and staple in place about 25 mm from the top of the timber rail of the seat (see page 28.) Use a sharp section of your trimming knife to trim the foam close to the staples.

COVERING THE CHAIR
13 Measure, cut and fit the cover (see page 18) and stretch it on the seat (see page 28). If there is a dressed timber edge on the bottom of the

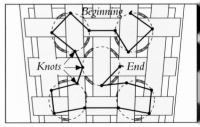

6 Sew the springs into place with your packing needle and jute twine, starting and ending with a slip knot.

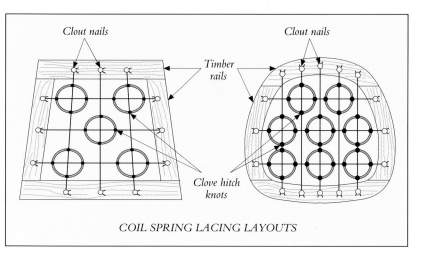

COIL SPRING LACING LAYOUTS

seat, staple the cover next to the timber. Make cuts in the cover to fit it around the chair legs (see page 41).

14 Finish the front corners of the seat with double pleats (see page 29), and staple the pleats on the chair sides close to the timber edge. Trim the excess fabric 2 mm from the staples using a sharp trimming knife.

CONTINUOUS STUDDING
15 Start from the back leg and butt the studding strip next to the dressed timber edge. Using a tack hammer with masking tape over the head as a softener, hammer a tack in the first hole of the strip. Pull the strip to the next corner, stretching it a little, and hammer a tack in the corner hole. Fill the holes of the strip with studs.
● To join two strips, place the end holes of each strip together and hammer a stud through both holes.
● To end, cut off the excess studding

using side cutters to the last hole and hammer a stud into the last hole. Finish the remaining area with a few single studs.

FINISHING THE CHAIR
16 Finish the chair with calico stretched under the base of the seat (see page 31).

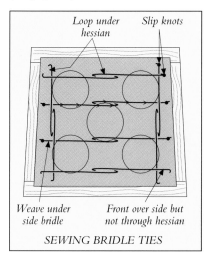

SEWING BRIDLE TIES

A contemporary blue cover complements the dark timber frame of this bridge chair. The swivelling back rest is removed from the frame for re-covering and finished with single pleats for a smooth and tidy appearance.

Bridge chair

The techniques used for re-covering a chair with a back rest are the same ones used for replacing a seat. The cover is fitted around the chair legs with a series of small cuts and the fabric panels are attached with back tacking and slip stitching.

REQUIREMENTS★

- Jute webbing: 6.5 m
- Jute twine (for sewing springs)
- Cotton piping (for lacing springs)
- 18 ounce hessian: 1 m
- 10 mm plastic edging roll: 0.5 m
- Fibre: 1.5 kg
- Foam (for seat and back): 25 mm thick, grade #24–160
- Foam (for back): 25 mm thick, grade #15–60
- Fabric: 1.5 m
- Back tack strip (for outside back)
- Slip-stitching twine
- Calico: 0.5 m
- Staples or tacks

★ Quantities given are for this particular chair.

PREPARATION

1 Strip the old upholstery off the seat and back rest (see page 12).

2 To remove the swivelling back rest from the frame of the chair, use a suitable-sized spanner to loosen the holding bolts. Check the chair frame and repair it if necessary (refer to page 14).

THE SEAT FOUNDATIONS

3 Depending on the condition of the seat foundations in your individual chair, you may need to replace the coil springs, webbing, hessian, foam, fibre and/or edging roll (see instructions on page 36).

THE BACK FOUNDATIONS

4 Attach three lengths of jute webbing vertically on the front of the back rest frame and two interlaced webs horizontally across the frame. Stretch the hessian tightly over the jute webbing (see page 28). Trim the hessian and fold back the edges before stapling into place.

5 Trim the hard foam (grade #24-160) for the back rest so that it is the same size as the frame and does not

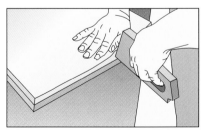

5 Trim the hard foam (grade #24-160) for the back rest so that it is the same size as the frame.

roll over the edges. Attach the foam to the frame but don't staple through the whole 25 mm thickness of foam. Instead, push back the side of the foam, catch about half the thickness and staple it to the frame.

6 Trim the second piece of foam (grade #15-60) for the back rest, making allowances on the top edge for the foam to roll over the top of the frame. Place it over the first piece and staple it along the bottom of the frame. Stretch the foam over the top of the frame and staple it to the back of the top edge.

7 Using your trimming knife, trim the soft foam so there is an 8 mm overhang on the sides of the frame and trim the bottom and top edges of the foam close to the staples.

COVERING THE SEAT
8 Measure the chair panels and cut and fit the new fabric (see page 18). Stretch the new covers on the seat. When covering the chair, lay it in a comfortable position as you work on each section.

9 Once the cover is stretched on the seat, pull the fabric to the corner close to the chair leg, hold one finger inside the fold, and lay the fabric flat to the seat.

10 Using scissors, cut from the corner of the fabric diagonally towards the timber leg, stopping at least 25 mm away from the leg. Stretch the fabric around the leg and check the cut. If a closer cut is required, pull the fabric out of the leg area and cut a bit further. It is better to have to make a number of small cuts than to cut too much.

11 Pull the fabric back down around the chair leg and trim off the excess fabric at each side of the leg. Make sure that you leave only enough fabric for it to be folded back beside the timber leg.

12 Fold the fabric under next to the chair leg. Stretch the fold under the frame and staple close any open areas next to the corner of the side. Repeat for all corners where the cover needs to be fitted around a leg

9 Pull the fabric to the corner, hold one finger inside the fold, and lay the fabric flat to the seat.

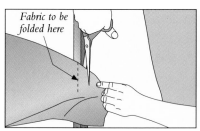

Fabric to be folded here

11 Pull the fabric back down around the leg and trim off the excess fabric at each side of the leg.

SINGLE-PLEATED CORNERS

1 Stretch the fabric at the top of one side up and over the corner of the frame. Staple the fabric on the outside of the frame.

2 Staple the side area of the inside back and fold a small pleat near the top corner. This pleat should only be seen at the back of the frame. Using scissors, trim any excess fabric from the side of the back rest and cut around the staple on the top edge. Hold the excess fabric over the frame and cut away any fabric not needed for the pleat on the top of the back rest.

3 Fold the fabric so that the top edge of the back rest has a neat, tight, single pleat and staple the fabric on the outside of the frame.

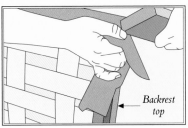

1 Stretch the fabric at the top of one side up and over the corner of the frame. Staple to the outside.

2 Staple the side area of the inside back and fold a small pleat near the top corner.

or rail. Trim off the excess fabric from the underside of the seat.

13 Attach a calico dust cover (see page 31) to the underside of the seat.

COVERING THE BACK
14 Stretch the inside back fabric panel on the chair back and attach all the sides with staples. Finish the corners with single pleats.

15 Reassemble the chair back. Use a trimming knife to make a small cut in the fabric to push the bolt through. Place a lock nut over the

first nut otherwise the back will work its way loose. The back rest should swivel, so do not over-tighten the nuts.

16 Position the outside back fabric panel on the chair back. Back-tack the top of the outside back panel to the top of the back rest frame (see back-tacking instructions on page 33). Staple the bottom edge of the outside back to the underside of the back rest frame. Fold the side edges under and slip stitch the sides of the outside back where it joins the inside back panel (see page 25).

When upholstering older-style furniture, it is important to choose a fabric, such as this jacquard, that suits the period of the piece. This chair has been finished with buttons and gimp to complement its classic style.

Nursing chair

This antique-style chair, with its elegant shape, requires more advanced fitting techniques than chairs with simple lines, but it is still easily upholstered using modern techniques. Small pleats are used to ease the cover around the curves of the chair back.

PREPARATION

1 Measure the panels, including an allowance for new stuffing, and cut the fabric (see page 18). The chair seat will be removed before the inside back is re-covered, but you should measure and cut all the fabric panels while the seat is still in place.

2 Strip the covers and foundations off the seat until only the timber frame is left. Remove the old fabric covers from the back rest. Check the chair frame and repair it if necessary (see page 14).

THE INSIDE BACK

3 Stretch the 12 mm thick piece of foam on the inside back (see page 28). Do not pull the foam around the small arm extensions which are covered separately.

4 Fit the inside back fabric panel on the chair back and make two cuts in the bottom of the fabric to go around the timber rail supports. Temporarily staple the inside back fabric following the diagram on page 46. Attach the base edge of the inside back with staples, but do not staple the corners.

REQUIREMENTS★

● Jute webbing: 4 m
● Jute twine and cotton piping
● 18 ounce hessian: 1 m
● 25 mm paper edging roll: 1.2 m
● Fibre: 1.5 kg
● Foam (for seat): 25 mm thick, grade #24–160
● Foam (for back): 12 mm thick, grade #20–130
● 200 g polyester wadding: 1 m
● Fabric: 2 m
● Slip-stitching twine
● Six buttons: size 32
● Calico: 0.5 m
● Staples or tacks

★ Quantities given are for this particular chair.

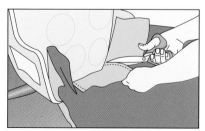

4 Fit the inside back panel and make two cuts at the bottom of the fabric to go around the timber rail supports.

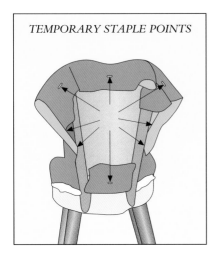

TEMPORARY STAPLE POINTS

the inside back panel, pull the folded section tightly over the inside back panel and attach with two staples to the timber on the outside back.

9 Place small cuts in the fabric on the underside of the small arm so it can be stretched around the rail support. Pull the fabric to the front of the small arm and staple on the outside back. Finish off the small arms with small pleats, making sure no pleating shows on the front of the chair and that all stapling will be covered by the outside back panel.

5 Stretch the cover firmly over the top of the inside back and permanently staple the top side.

6 Staple the sides of the inside back. A series of small cuts in the fabric will allow you to follow the concave shape of the sides. Work from the centre of the concave shape to the outsides of the shape on each side.

7 Finish the top corners of the inside back with a series of small pleats to ease the fullness of the cover around the top corners. These pleats should not extend to the front of the chair and should not be visible once the outside back panel is attached. Staple the pleats into place. Trim off the excess fabric.

8 Stretch small pieces of 12 mm thick foam over the small arm areas that extend from the inside back. Fold the fabric under on the side that meets

10 Slip stitch the folded side of the small arm cover to the inside back panel (see page 25). Trim off the excess fabric and finish off the inside back panel with buttons.

COVERING THE SEAT

11 If your project requires it, replace the foundations and the stuffing in the chair seat (see page 36), as well as the edging roll on the front and sides.

12 Fit the fabric seat panel to the seat and place cuts in the fabric

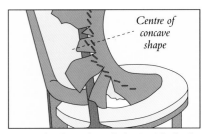

Centre of concave shape

6 Staple the sides of the inside back. Use small cuts in the fabric to follow the concave shape.

FINISHING WITH BUTTONS

Buttoning is a decorative finish on large upholstered panels but it is also used to hold cushions in place. Upholstery buttons are usually made of metal components and covered in fabric—you will need a local upholsterer to make them.

1 Measure the button positions either by duplicating the original button layout or by placing them in a position of your choice. Mark the button positions with skewers. Cut a length of jute twine about 800 mm long. Thread a single end of the twine through the loop at the back of the button, then thread the two ends of the twine through the hole of a straight needle.

2 Remove the skewer and place the end of the needle into the skewer hole. Pull the needle

through the stuffing to the back of the panel.

3 Place a second button on one side only of the twine. Tie a slip knot (see page 61) with the button inside the knotted area and pull the knot until the button is positioned to the desired depth.

4 Tie two finishing knots and cut off the excess thread.

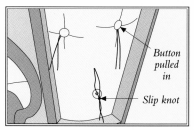

3 Place a second button on one side only of the twine. Tie a slip knot in the twine.

wherever it needs to be stretched around a timber rail. Do not cut the fabric right to the rail—stop about

25 mm from the rail and check the fit before doing any fine-tune cutting (see page 41).

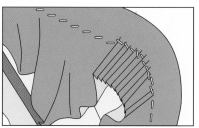

7 Finish the top corner with a series of small pleats to ease the fullness of the cover around the corners.

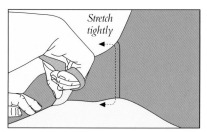

9 Place small cuts in the fabric on the underside of the small arm so it can be stretched around the rail support.

This chair seat needed new coil springs, but the back rest foundations were in good condition.

13 Stretch the cover on the seat (see page 28), staple to the underside and finish the front corners with large single pleats (see opposite).

THE OUTSIDE BACK

14 Stretch hessian over the outside back. Trim the polyester wadding to shape so that it is 10 mm inside the edges of the outside back panel. Attach the wadding with five or six staples in the centre of each side and one staple on the outside of each of the small arm extensions.

15 Temporarily attach the outside back panel to the chair back with skewers or pins and trim the panel to the shape of the sides and top. Make sure you leave enough fabric to fold under for slip stitching (about 25 mm allowance on all sides).

16 Fold the fabric under on the sides and top of the outside back and pin the cover to the shape of the chair. Slip stitch the outside back panel to the inside back. Start stitching from the centre of the top of the chair and work across the top and down one side. Pull out the pins as you go. Repeat the slip stitch on the other side of the outside back, again starting from the centre of the top and working across the top of the chair and down the side.

17 Release the temporary holding point at the bottom of the outside back cover and staple the bottom of the outside back cover to the underside of the chair. Trim the excess fabric from the underside of the chair.

FINISHING WITH GIMP

If a chair has a decorative timber strip, the raw edges of the fabric cover can be finished with gimp. Alternatively, you can choose to finish the raw edges with double piping or continuous studding.

18 With the wrong side facing you, start the gimp under the seat of the chair behind the front leg. Staple the end of the gimp in place, then fold it over to hide the staple. (This is a similar technique to back-tacking, see page 33).

19 With a pre-heated hot-glue gun, put two thin lines of melted glue on the wrong side of the gimp and push

LARGE SINGLE PLEATS

Use this technique for any upholstery project that is finished with large single pleats. It is essential to close large pleats with studs or slip stitching so the fold will not open.

1 Pull the fabric over the corner of the seat and staple the side of the panel to the front edge of the chair.

2 Cut the fabric beside the staples, pull the excess past the front edge of the chair and cut off the extra fabric leaving enough fabric to fold inside the pleat.

3 Pull the pleat down tightly and staple. Close the pleat with slip stitching (see page 25). Trim off the excess fabric from under the seat.

1 Pull the fabric over the corner of the seat and staple the side of the panel to the front edge of the chair.

2 Cut the fabric beside the staples, pull the excess past the front edge of the chair and trim the extra fabric.

the gimp into place. Work across the front of the chair towards the other side, working in small sections so the glue will stay melted while you position the gimp.

20 Finish by stapling the end of the gimp under the seat. If the gimp is to be joined, stop about 40 mm from the end and work out where the ends will meet. Cut off the excess gimp, leaving 12 mm to turn under. Place a small dot of hot glue on the reverse side at the end and fold the 12 mm of excess gimp under. Glue the remaining end of gimp in place.

FINISHING THE CHAIR

21 Cut out a piece of calico to use as a dust cover and attach it to the underside of the chair seat with staples (see page 31).

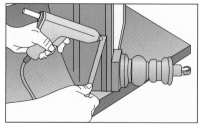

19 Place two thin lines of melted glue on the reverse side of the gimp and push the gimp into position.

Occasional tub chair

Chairs with fully upholstered panels require careful preparation of the fabric covers and attention to fitting and sewing. The foundations of this chair were in good condition and did not need replacing, so an extra layer of foam was added for comfort.

PREPARATION

1 Carefully remove the fabric covers from the entire chair (see page 12). If you are replacing the foundations on the back and arms, strip them off. Remove the existing wadding from the seat and place it aside, but don't remove the foundations if they don't need repair. If you do need to replace the foundations of the chair seat, refer to the instructions for coil spring seats on page 36. Check the frame and repair it if necessary.

2 For reinforcement, attach extra English webbing to the underside of the chair on top of the old webbing.

3 Stretch and staple new hessian over the seat springs to protect the new covers from any dust that may be on

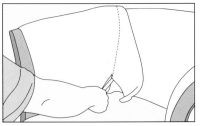

4 Prepare the inside back and arms for covering by attaching the 12 mm thick foam over the old stuffing.

REQUIREMENTS★

- Jute webbing: 5 m
- Jute twine and cotton piping (for lacing and sewing springs)
- 18 ounce hessian: 2 m
- Felt: 1 m
- Foam (for back): 12 mm thick, grade #20-130
- Foam (for arms): 12 mm thick, grade #20-130
- 200 g polyester wadding: 1 m
- Fabric: 3.5 m
- Four back tack strips: 12 mm wide
- Calico: 1 m
- Staples or tacks

★ Quantities given are for this particular chair.

the springs. Sew the springs to the hessian (see page 36) and sew new bridle ties if necessary.

4 Cut and stretch the new 12 mm thick foam over the old stuffing. Attach the foam with staples but do not staple the foam where the inside arms join the inside back. Instead, cut the foam to size and position the pieces to fit without overlapping.

A subtle, elegant fabric complements the shape of this chair without detracting from the decorative timber. The double piping finish enhances the smooth lines of the chair, as well as hiding the raw edge of the fabric covers.

5 Measure the chair panels and cut out the fabric covers (see page 18). Fit the fabric panels to the chair. Sew together the pieces that make up the front border panel, and measure and sew the double piping for finishing off the chair (see page 55).

THE INSIDE BACK AND INSIDE ARMS

6 Sew the inside back panel to the inside arm panels. These seams should be piped for reinforcement because you will need to use a lot of tension when pulling these seams into place and attaching them to the chair. (See Piped seams, page 26.)

7 Lay the sewn panels on the inside back and the arms, and place cuts in the fabric beside the piping where the covers need to be pulled around the timber rails (see page 41).

8 Attach the bottom ends of the piping to the rails at the back of the chair with staples. Stretch the piped joins tightly up and over the top of the chair frame and staple the piping to the outside of the chair.

9 Staple the top and bottom edges of the inside back panel to the outside of the chair frame.

10 Attach the inside arm panels, first at the top and bottom, then at the side near the front timber rail. When finishing off next to the decorative timber at the front of the arms, keep the staples as straight as possible and approximately 2 mm back from the timber. You do not need to attach the sides that have piping joins.

11 Trim the excess fabric next to the timber arm fronts using a new section of your trimming knife. Then trim any excess fabric from the rest of the inside covering.

THE SEAT

12 Replace the original stuffing on the seat or repad the foundation. Fill any holes in the old stuffing by adding fibre or felt until the seat feels even. Add a full layer of felt over the whole seat as extra padding.

13 Fit the fabric panel on the seat and place cuts in the fabric where it

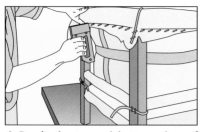

9 Staple the top and bottom edges of the inside back panel to the outside of the chair frame.

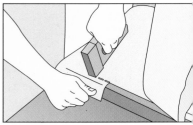

10 Attach the inside arm panels, first at the top and bottom and then at the side near the timber front rail.

needs to go around the timber support rails. Stretch the seat cover over the seat area, making sure that you pull the fabric down firmly to squash the felt flat (see page 28). Staple to the horizontal timber rail.

14 Finish the front corners of the seat with a single pleat (see page 43) and trim off any excess fabric from the seat of the chair.

THE FRONT BORDER

15 The front border should be already sewn in your preparation for covering. Back-tack the top of the front border to the horizontal timber rail at the front of the chair seat. (Refer to the instructions for back-tacking on page 33.)

16 Turn back the front border so that you can staple a piece of hessian on the chair front underneath where the border will be. Then staple a piece of polyester wadding under the front border and over the hessian. Pull the border back down and staple the base and sides close to the decorative timber strip.

Be careful when stapling or tacking close to decorative timber. It is very easy to bruise the timber accidentally.

THE OUTSIDE BACK

17 Prepare the outside covers by fitting the outside back panel and the outside arm panels to the chair and pinning and machine-sewing the panels together. Once satisfied with the fit of the entire outside back cover, pin the cover to the chair and then pull the cover to the inside of the chair so the top raw edge is visible. Using four or five staples, attach the top of the outside back and arm panels along the raw edge.

18 Staple the back tack strips over the top of the raw edge of the fabric

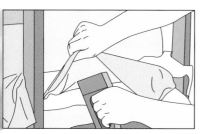

13 Stretch the seat cover on the chair seat, and staple it to the horizontal timber rail.

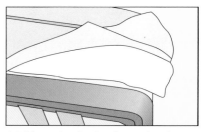

16 Turn back the front border to attach the hessian. Staple polyester wadding under the front border.

Double piping is an elegant finish that is becoming increasingly popular in upholstered furniture.

cover to create a clean edge for back-tacking. Make sure the back tack strips are evenly placed around the top of the chair.

19 Cover the entire outside area of the chair with hessian. Fold back the edge to avoid fraying and staple the top of the hessian over the back tack strips. Stretch the hessian evenly over the outside of the chair, fold back the edges and attach with staples at the top and bottom of the chair and next to the decorative timber strip on the sides of the chair.

20 Measure and cut the polyester wadding. If you need to join the wadding so that it will go around the outside of the chair, butt the edges together. Do not overlap the wadding as this causes an unsightly bump under the cover. Attach the wadding over the hessian with 8–10 staples and trim off any excess wadding.

21 Pull the outside cover back down over the wadding and make sure it is stretched evenly and the cover fits neatly. Starting from the centre, attach the base of the outside back cover with staples. Then staple the base of the outside arms and finally the sides of the outside arms approximately 1–2 mm away from the decorative timber strip.

22 Trim the excess fabric next to the decorative timber strip with a sharp trimming knife.

FINISHING

23 Finish off the chair with double piping around the timber rails and attach a piece of calico on the underside of the chair (see page 31).

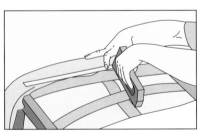

18 Staple back tack strips over the top of the fabric to create a clean edge for the back-tacking.

19 Cover the outside area with hessian. Staple the hessian over the back tack strip and stretch it tightly.

DOUBLE PIPING

Double-piping fabric strips should be at least 65 mm wide. Some fabrics may be too heavy for double piping, so try sewing a sample first.

1 Cut two pieces of cotton piping about 100 mm longer than the length required. Sew one 'cord' inside the piping fabric. Turn the fabric around the second cord so both the pieces are covered and the right side of the fabric faces you. Sew between the two cotton piping cords, being careful not to catch them. Trim the excess fabric to 2 mm from the stitching.

2 To attach, undo the first few stitches and cut 12 mm off both cords. Fold the excess fabric to the underside of the double piping.

3 Position one end of the piping at the starting point and staple between the cords and over the stitch line with a long staple. You may need to tap the staple with a

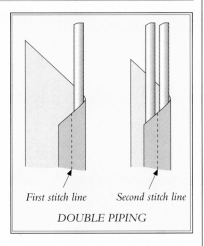

First stitch line   Second stitch line

DOUBLE PIPING

hammer to close the piping neatly and make sure the staple is holding.

4 Using a pre-heated hot-glue gun, put a thick line of glue over the stitch line on the wrong side and push the piping into place. Firmly run a regulator over the stitch line to close the piping cords together. Work in small sections so the glue stays melted. To end, reverse the procedures of steps 2 and 3.

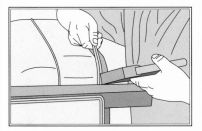

3 Position one end of the piping at the starting point and staple between the two piping cords.

4 Using a pre-heated hot-glue gun, put a thick line of glue over the stitch line on the wrong side.

The zigzag spring foundation of this chair was in good condition and did not need repair, so new rubber webbing was added to strengthen it. Polyester wadding was placed over the existing stuffing of the entire chair for comfort.

Wingback chair

Wingback chairs with their classic curves and many elements are not as difficult to upholster as they may seem. Success depends on attention to fitting and sewing the covers, so keep the old fabric panels as they will be a useful guide.

PREPARATION

1 Remove the upholstery, keeping the old covers as intact as possible. At the same time, measure up and cut the new fabric, including the skirt and cushion panels, using the old covers as patterns. Copy the finishing details (for example, piped seams and pleats) on to your new covers. Remove the arm facings very carefully as they are usually made of thin pieces of timber. Prise them off with a screwdriver or ripping chisel.

2 Sew all the fabric panels which require stitching, referring to the sewing techniques on pages 22–7. You should also sew up any piping.

3 Check the chair frame and make any necessary repairs (see page 14).

4 Replace or repair the foundations if required. Some wingback chairs have coil spring seats (see page 36), while others, like this one, have zigzag spring foundations (see page 62). The zigzag springs did not need replacement so new rubber webbing was interlaced with the existing springs to reinforce and strengthen the seat foundation.

REQUIREMENTS★

- Fabric: 7 m
- 200 g polyester wadding: 6 m
- Back tack strip: 12 mm wide
- Calico: 1 m
- Slip-stitching twine
- Staples or tacks
- Buttons
- Rubber webbing: 3 m
- Zigzag springs cut to size (optional): use a firm grade, e.g. 9 or 10 gauge, for seat foundations
- Zigzag spring clips (optional)
- 5 mm clout nails (optional)
- Cotton piping (optional)
- 18 ounce hessian (optional)

★ Quantities given are for this particular chair.

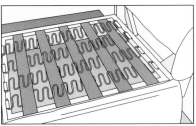

4 Interlace new rubber webbing with the existing springs to reinforce them and strengthen the seat foundation.

5 Cut and fit the polyester wadding to cover the outside of the entire chair. Stretch the wadding over the existing foundations and attach with staples. Do not overlap the wadding where the panels meet. Instead, butt the pieces together for an even finish.

COVERING THE INSIDE
Cover the inside panels of the wingback chair in the following order using the general stretching techniques on pages 28–9.

6 Stretch the inside arm panel over one inside arm area and staple to the outside. Make small cuts in the fabric to fit it around the curved shape of the arm. Use a series of small pleats, about five to seven pleats should be enough, to ease the cover around the curved top on the chair arm and staple the pleats in place (see page 46). Repeat for the other inside arm.

7 Stretch the under seat panel over the under seat area and attach with staples. Make small cuts in the fabric if the cover has to be pulled around any timber rails (see page 41).

8 Attach the front border panel to the front of the chair. The top of the panel should be back-tacked to the under seat fabric panel and the sides and base of the front border panel should be stapled to the timber rails of the chair.

9 Stretch the inside wing panel over the inside wing area and staple to the outside. Use a series of small pleats to fit the cover around the curves at the top of the wing. These pleats should not be seen when the outside back of the chair is covered. Repeat to cover the other inside wing panel.

10 Stretch the inside back fabric panel over the inside back of the chair. You will need to pull the edges of the cover around the inside back to the outside of the chair frame and attach with staples to the timber rail.

BUTTONING
11 Attach the buttons to the inside back (see instructions on page 47).
• Mark the button positions on the inside back with skewers or pins.
• Thread a needle with jute twine and

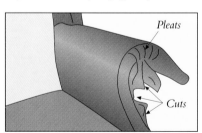

6 Stretch the inside arm panel over one arm. Use a series of small pleats to fit the cover around the curve.

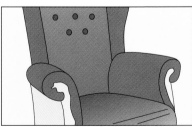

11 Mark the button positions with skewers or pins and attach the buttons to the inside back.

thread the twine through the back of the button.

- Remove the skewer and pull the needle from the front of the inside back to the outside.
- Place a second button on the twine and tie a slip knot (see page 61). Pull the knot until the button is at the right depth, tie two finishing knots and cut off the excess thread.

COVERING THE OUTSIDE

All the outside panels of the chair should be attached using the general stretching directions, but they should also be back-tacked at the top of the panel (see page 33) and slip stitched on the sides (see page 25).

12 Stretch the fabric panel over one outside wing of the chair. Back-tack the top of the outside wing panel with some back tack strip cut to size. Staple the back edge of the outside wing panel to the outside of the chair frame. Then staple the base of the panel to the chair frame. Slip stitch the front of the outside wing panel to the inside wing. Repeat for the other outside wing.

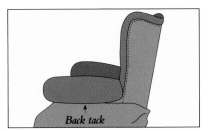

Back tack

13 Stretch the fabric panel on the outside arm and back-tack the top of the panel.

PANEL PINS

Panel pins are metal nails with a very small tapered head that allows the pins to pass through fabric threads and behind the fabric so that they are not visible. Panel pins come in various sizes— 40 mm is the most common in upholstery—and they are available from hardware stores and upholstery suppliers.

13 Stretch the outside arm fabric panel over one outside arm area and back-tack the top of the panel. Staple the base of the panel to the chair frame under the outside arm and staple the back of the panel to the outside back of the chair. The front of the outside arm panel should be stapled to the arm facing area.

14 Back-tack the top of the outside back panel to attach it. Staple the base of the panel to the underside of the chair. Fold the fabric under on the sides and pin the fold to the outside wing and outside arm fabric panels. Slip stitch the sides of the outside back.

THE ARM FACINGS

15 Stretch the arm facing panel over one of the arm facings and attach to the back of the facing piece with small staples or tacks approximately 4 mm in length. Alternatively, you can use contact adhesive in a spray can to glue the fabric in place.

16 Using panel pins and a tack hammer, re-attach the facings to the chair arm. Make sure you place the head of the panel pin between the fabric threads of the cover before hammering it in. Depending on the size of the arm facing on your chair, it will take about seven to ten panel pins to secure the facing but you should only use just enough pins to hold the facing in place.

ATTACHING THE SKIRT

17 Sew the new skirt using the old fabric as a pattern and refer to the sewing techniques on pages 22–7, and the following instructions.

• Measure the finished size of the old skirt. Cut out the front, back and two side pieces, then the four corner pieces from the new fabric. Include a 25 mm hemming allowance on the sides and bottom of every piece and a sewing allowance of 12 mm at the top of every piece.

• Sew the hems on all skirt pieces.

• Stitch the piping for the skirt, making sure there is enough to go around the chair with an allowance of approximately 150 mm.

• Sew the piping to the top of the skirt panels beginning with the back piece, then a side piece, next the front piece and finally the other side piece. When you reach the end of each panel, butt the next panel up to it with the corner piece placed under the two skirt panels. Do not join the last side piece with the back, rather leave that corner open at this stage.

18 With the chair upright and the legs replaced if you have removed them, attach the skirt from underneath with staples (this is a similar technique to back-tacking) so that the skirt is no more than 25 mm off the ground. Start at the back of the chair, work your away around and stop attaching about 75 mm from the open corner of the skirt.

19 Turn the chair upside down again to finish off the piping at the open corner of the skirt. Unpick a few of the stitches joining the skirt panels to the piping, and finish the piping by sewing the ends together by hand (see page 27) or joining and stapling the ends to the chair frame.

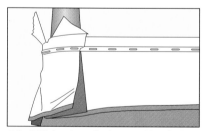

20 With the chair upside down, staple the side and back pieces on the piping, then staple the corner piece.

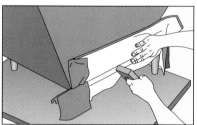

21 Butt the back tack strips up to the edge of the piping around the whole skirt and staple.

20 With the chair upside down, close off the open corner of the skirt. Staple the side and back panels of the skirt over the piping, then staple the corner piece over the panels.

21 Butt the back tack strips up to the edge of the piping around the whole skirt (as you would for back-tacking) and staple into place using long staples or 16 mm tacks.

22 Unscrew the legs again, and attach calico to the base of the chair. Pull the calico to the sides of the chair, fold the edges under and staple over the top of the back tack strips used to back tack the skirt. Reattach the legs, turn the chair right side up.

THE SEAT CUSHION

When making a separate cushion for a chair, use the old fabric as a pattern and refer to the instructions for a fully piped cushion on page 27.

23 Sew the cushion in this order. Join the piping to each of the face panels. Sew the zip fastener to the border panel. Attach the border to one of the face panels and trim off any excess border fabric. Sew the other face panel to the border. Turn the cushion cover the right way out and check the seams.

24 Filling can be tricky in some cases, so use the following method.
• Fold the foam in half and hold the foam about one third of the way back from the front.

SLIP KNOTS

Slip knots are the most commonly used knots in upholstery. For example, they are used to sew springs to hessian (as in the diagram below) and also to attach buttons to chair panels. Use a circular needle and jute twine when sewing slip knots in foundations, and a long needle and jute twine for buttoning.

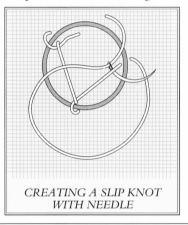

*CREATING A SLIP KNOT
WITH NEEDLE*

• Slip the cushion cover over the folded foam.
• Push the foam up into the cover as far as it will go, then re-grip the foam towards the back of it and push the back half into the cushion cover.
• Push the two front corners of the foam into the front corners of the cover, then push the back corners of the foam into place.
• Work the foam straight (i.e. unfold it) while also pushing the foam to the front of the cover.
• When satisfied, zip the cushion up.

REPLACING ZIGZAG SPRINGS

This type of foundation consists of a continuous, metal spring wire shaped into a zigzag layout.

1 Strip off the old stuffing and hessian (see page 12). Remove the old springs using a lever such as a screwdriver and mallet.

2 Attach a new zigzag spring clip with the clout nails, leaving the folded end of the clip 5 mm over the timber edge to the inside of the frame. Attach another clip to the opposite side of the seat to hold the other end of the zigzag spring.

3 Place one side of the spring into the clip and close the clip by tapping it with a medium-sized hammer. Hammer clout nails into the holes of the clip to secure it.

4 Pull the spring to the opposing clip and place it in the fold of the

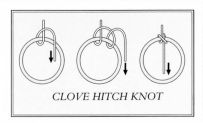

CLOVE HITCH KNOT

clip. Tap the clip with the hammer to close it and finish off by securing it with clout nails. Repeat steps 2 to 4 for each zigzag spring.

5 On chair seats with more than three springs, lace cotton piping across the springs so that they won't spread apart when sat on. Start the lacing on one side by tying the cord to a clout nail, then hit the clout nail all the way in with the medium-sized hammer. Tie the cord to each spring with a clove hitch knot (see diagram) before finishing the lacing on the opposite side with another clout nail. Hammer the clout nail into the timber rail after the knot is tied.

6 Cover the springs with hessian, leaving it loose to compensate for sagging when the seat is used. Staple the hessian on all sides and trim it to 30 mm from the staples.

7 Turn over the raw edges of the hessian to prevent it fraying at the sides and place more staples on top to finish the seat foundation.

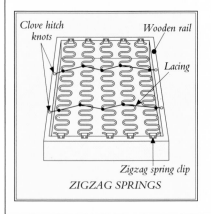

Clove hitch knots

Wooden rail

Lacing

Zigzag spring clip

ZIGZAG SPRINGS

Tools for upholstery

Some of the most useful tools for upholstery are shown below. Build up your tool kit gradually—most tools can be purchased from your local hardware store or upholstery supplier.

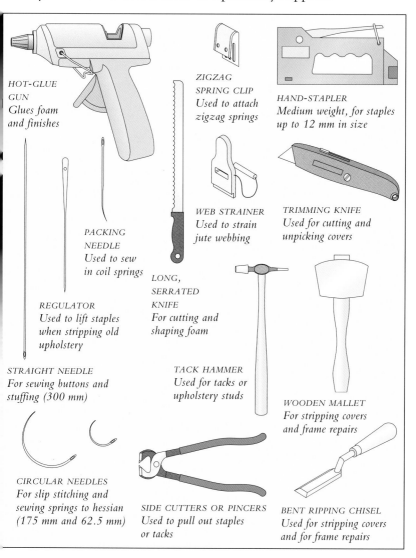

HOT-GLUE GUN
Glues foam and finishes

ZIGZAG SPRING CLIP
Used to attach zigzag springs

HAND-STAPLER
Medium weight, for staples up to 12 mm in size

PACKING NEEDLE
Used to sew in coil springs

WEB STRAINER
Used to strain jute webbing

TRIMMING KNIFE
Used for cutting and unpicking covers

LONG, SERRATED KNIFE
For cutting and shaping foam

REGULATOR
Used to lift staples when stripping old upholstery

STRAIGHT NEEDLE
For sewing buttons and stuffing (300 mm)

TACK HAMMER
Used for tacks or upholstery studs

WOODEN MALLET
For stripping covers and frame repairs

CIRCULAR NEEDLES
For slip stitching and sewing springs to hessian (175 mm and 62.5 mm)

SIDE CUTTERS OR PINCERS
Used to pull out staples or tacks

BENT RIPPING CHISEL
Used for stripping covers and for frame repairs

Index